CW01197558

*Also by Bobby Parker*

*Blue Movie* (Nine Arches, 2014)

*Working Class Voodoo* (Offord Road Books, 2018)

*Resurrection Mary* (Secret Sleep Books, 2021)

# HONEY MONSTER

## *Parker*

If you're feeling like you want to die, it's important to tell someone. Help and support is available right now if you need it. You do not have to struggle with difficult feelings alone.

### Phone a free helpline

SAMARITANS / 116 123 / jo@samaritans.org

CALM / 0800 58 58 58 / 5pm to midnight

PAPYRUS – under 35y/o / 0800 068 41 41 / 9am to midnight / Text 07860 039967 / pat@papyrus-uk.org

CHILDLINE – under 19y/o / 0800 1111 – won't show up on phone bill

SOS / 0300 1020 505 / 4pm - midnight / support@sossilenceofsuicide.org

### Message a text line

Shout Crisis Text Line / Text "SHOUT" to 85258

YoungMinds / for people under 19 / Text "YM" to 85258

### Talk to someone you trust

Let family or friends know what's going on for you. They may be able to offer support and help keep you safe. There's no right or wrong way to talk about suicidal feelings – starting the conversation is what's important.

### Who else you can talk to

call a GP – ask for an emergency appointment

call 111 out of hours – they will help you find support and help

contact your mental health crisis team – if you have one

### Is your life in danger?

If you have seriously harmed yourself – for example, by taking a drug overdose – or you feel that you may be about to harm yourself, call 999 for an ambulance or go straight to A&E. Or ask someone else to call 999 or take you to A&E.

© Bobby Parker, 2022. All rights reserved; no part of this book may be reproduced by any means without the publisher's permission.

ISBN: 978-1-913642-83-9

The author/s has asserted their right to be identified as the author of this Work in accordance with the Copyright, Designs and Patents Act 1988

Cover design by Aaron Kent

Edited & typeset by Aaron Kent

Broken Sleep Books (2021)

Broken Sleep Books Ltd
Rhydwen,
Talgarreg,
SA44 4HB
Wales

## *Contents*

| | |
|---|---|
| Floating in the Harbour | 11 |
| The Red Child | 13 |
| Salvia Divinorum is the Devil | 14 |
| Things I talk about when I've taken my sleeping pills | 15 |
| Citizen | 16 |
| Spooky Jeans | 17 |
| Beavis & Butthead | 20 |
| Sticky Legs | 21 |
| This Poem Will Make You Rich | 22 |
| I'm Going Over the Fence | 23 |
| Ramble On | 24 |
| Three Months Sober (and it's almost Halloween) | 25 |
| Skin Past Bone | 27 |
| Midnight Snack | 36 |
| Come Down (Three Bad Dreams) | 37 |
| Resurrection Mary | 40 |
| Wackadoodle | 66 |
| Eight Lincolnshire Sausages | 68 |
| Punxsutawney Phil Predicts an Early Spring | 70 |
| Power Cut | 71 |
| Scum of the Earth | 73 |
| The State of Sunday | 74 |
| MEN WITH VEN | 76 |
| Night of the Creeps | 77 |
| Catfish Gumbo | 78 |
| Bottomless Roast | 79 |

| | |
|---|---|
| The White Flame | 81 |
| Revenge is a Dish Best Served Bald | 82 |
| A Haunting in Kidderminster | 84 |
| Honey Monster | 85 |
| Zippo | 124 |
| | |
| Acknowledgements | 131 |

*For Katy
and
Isobelle*

*God will forgive them. He'll forgive them and allow them into Heaven. I can't live with that.*
— Dead Man's Shoes

*There are some nice people in the world, you know, I just don't happen to be related to any of them.*
— Little Edie (Grey Gardens, 1976)

*You cannot go poking skeletons in the closet without making maggots wriggle.*
— Salena Godden, Springfield Road

*Say, "I am sorry, forgive me," and a shower of reproaches will follow!*
— Dostoyevsky

*I'm making these bacon rolls real juicy dad…*
— The Greasy Strangler

# Honey Monster

**Bobby Parker**

## Content Warning:

Honey Monster contains writing and themes that some readers may find difficult to process, or traumatising.

## *Floating in the Harbour*

Six months before my daughter was born, my doctor introduced me to Benzodiazepines. Little did he know, they were my answer to everything. Within a couple of months I was buying them on the street. I discovered Xanax and Moggies. I felt like pink fog instead of rotting meat. Suddenly, life had cushions. It could be soft. Days passed like floating mattresses and from this angle my criminal friends seemed cartoonish, waving their silly knives about. When my ex-girlfriend's sister used our flat to hide her boyfriend, Chris (who was wanted for robbing post offices), it didn't bother me. He paid our bills and kept the fridge stocked with meat and cheese. We didn't have to use the food bank for the first time in six months. I didn't need to shoplift. Obviously, it was a bit disturbing when Chris left his gun on the kitchen table. But it just became another boring thing, like dropping your toothbrush or staring at an empty bus in the rain. I would move the gun to make room to butter the toast. I shoved it to one side with a pile of dirty plates like it was a teacup full of mould. One day I told Chris about a new dealer causing trouble on the estate, a rich boy called Trance. Trance didn't need to deal drugs, he just enjoyed doing it. I suppose it made him feel powerful. The night before my best mate died on his mother's living room floor, I told Trance that my buddy was in bad shape and not to sell anything to Rich. Trance told me to fuck off and hung up. I was still stewing over this as I carried Richard's coffin into the crematorium. As I placed one last spliff among the flowers. Chris grinned: if I really wanted revenge he would send a few boys round to rob this Trance fucker. He said I could have half the drugs or half the money. Chris was stretched across the battered blue sofa, hands behind his head. 'Just tell me his address...' He made it sound like stealing the neighbour's milk. I would be lying if I said I didn't consider it. I couldn't even be bothered to clean the filth from under my fingernails. Before I could make up my mind, Chris was caught red handed after he robbed another post office one week after leaving our place. This time he was the getaway driver. He got ten years in prison. It was good to have the place to ourselves again. I wasn't going to miss the sounds of him loudly banging her sister and sniffing coke all night listening to Gabba. Everything went back to normal. Except now we felt poorer than ever without Chris buying the food. I sold all my books and we unplugged the fridge to save electricity. I brushed off my long black thief coat. My ex-girlfriend's sister got into multi level marketing and tried to forget about her other life. Every Thursday the local Methodist church would make bacon sandwiches for the poor and homeless. Most of us in that cursed block of council flats, with its sad murders and prison-like corridors, looked forward to Thursdays - even Lucy, who said the volunteers couldn't fry eggs for shit. I remember staring at a pile of beat-up chess boards and worrying about my next move. I was going to be a daddy. When our baby kicked inside her mother's belly, it's horrible to say but I was too scared to touch it. Could I truly do what was expected of me? Is love even possible when your blood is all kinds of cloudy? My goodness, the promises I made... They were *this big*.

# *The Red Child*

I knew a boy whose parents gave him a white rat for his thirteenth birthday. The poor thing was blind, stinky and heavily pregnant. The boy was disgusted. He was hoping for a dirt bike. After she gave birth, the boy would rattle the cage to startle the nursing rat. Then he encouraged me to watch her kill and eat the babies. I remember dark pink slime dangled off her whiskers and we laughed so hard because it was strange and sad and because we thought that was love. I'm not sure if the rat sang a horrid gobbling squelching song as she devoured her litter, or whether I made it up after the boy disappeared. Either way, it's haunting me tonight. I'm dashed with sharp flint chippings in the topcoat of my render. Those council grey, chip fat houses. Baby teeth in old cement. Gorgeous, suffering, his eyes.

## *Salvia Divinorum is the Devil*

Lost near the river, I found my grandad. He was eating lifeless leaves from the trees. I asked him what he was doing. He said he was eating the leaves to get rid of the hunger. He told me the river was busy with death, which is why he was eating the leaves. I dangled my legs in the grandma-shaped hole where the flowers used to pop. His feet were too big. He told me that he hated the path because if he stepped on the grass he'd become poisoned again. I said 'What did it feel like?' He told me his beliefs were banned in every country. When he wasn't eating the leaves, he stared into the ugly water, hospital green with blue gowns waving under the rocks. I told him the river was deep and dangerous and that we should stop staring and build a shelter. He missed her so much, it was like the love they had was a monster now, a gremlin inside his faithful machine, and it stood on his tongue so it could look at the world through his eyes. I told him about my enemies, the ones I will crush when I'm enlightened. Smiling, he handed me a sticky red leaf. I ripped it in half. 'Let's share this one,' I said. Yes, I have a hard time out there, in my mind, I have swallowed it. Her big splash, behind us, our terrible laughter.

## *Things I talk about when I've taken my sleeping pills*

Did you know that Elvis and his friends would visit Memphis funeral homes in the middle of the night? This took place in the days leading up to his so-called death. There's something about that image. His painful hips, aviator sunglasses, baritone voice like a warm breeze among the caskets. That sleazy lip-curl and the King with all those peaceful bodies in the Bardo. Grease in his hair, flowers and formaldehyde. Do you think he was having a good time? Sure, Elvis was a prankster, but he was also curious about his loved ones' reactions if he died. I read that he hired an actor to shoot him with blanks while Elvis activated miniature explosive blood packs hidden under his famous sequinned jumpsuit. It's strange, the places we go to feel alive. I guess what I'm trying to say is that it's difficult to trust each other. Did you know that Elvis had a fear of penetration and liked women with tiny feet? He also owned an unbearable alcoholic chimpanzee called Coconut-headed Motherfucker. I know, baby… Don't worry. I'm scared too.

# *Citizen*
*for Lucy & Jason*

No matter how hard I try, I can't get the smell of blood off my fingers. I went to see my doctor, but she sniffed my hand so gently I almost burst into tears. I showed them to my angry mother, even though she had only just got back from the factory, and dad's cough is getting worse. I bought expensive soaps and fairground scented bath-bombs to soak in, but the steam turned me on and I got a bit distracted. I even tried getting so high my whole body didn't smell of anything at all, and it was glorious! But sure enough - when the drugs wore off - my soft hands smelled like blood again. Maybe there's something I must do to get rid of it. Who knows, this might be the spiritual adventure I've been waiting for. Have you listened to the sound of the wind on Mars? I use it to relax when all I can see is a picture of Earth on fire. It blows my mind to think about the people out there who don't beat themselves up about anything. I imagine their fingers smell like roast beef dinners and English gardens after the rain.

# *Spooky Jeans*

The girl who raped me had a really nice mum. Her name was Karen. She loved menthol cigarettes and wore Iron Maiden t-shirts. I liked her very much. Karen had a filthy motorbike and a teardrop tattoo. When the pubs closed we would all go to her place to drink white lightning until a fight broke out. Karen shared a house with her sister, Debbie, their ground floor windows boarded up and covered with graffiti. Debbie had been to prison for killing a woman in a drunken fight over a fake fur coat. Debbie would collapse on the floor and curse God while Karen danced and burned the pizzas. It was great. I enjoyed being around people as emotionally unstable as I was. One night, after everyone else had gone, Karen begged me to pretend to be her late husband. She wanted me to wear his old work clothes. His blue jeans, which were lovingly folded over the smelly armchair he would pass out in, frightened the piss out of me. She kept his steel toe boots by the front door, and whenever I passed them I felt a real sense of dread, like they resented me, and I would dream about untied laces during my worst hangovers. My diet was poor back then, I lived on chips and beans. I thought growing up in small houses, foggy with thick cigarette smoke, somehow fucked up my taste buds. But Karen introduced me to spaghetti Bolognese. She giggled when I burped so, of course, I would belch as deep and loud as I could, to make her happy. Sometimes I went too far and made myself sick. My mates found it funny when I told them what happened with Karen's daughter, like when I told them about Terry in the cornfield, or Jamie the babysitter, or Carl's dad with his vice-like grip: they said 'Why are people so fucking weird around you?' I told them Karen's daughter smelled like a seagull. I told them she dripped the stormy sea all over me. Ten years later I saw Karen's daughter smoking outside the local supermarket, blowing neat smoke rings just like her lovely mum used to. 'Hey! Remember me?' She said. 'I fucked you at Gary's party.' I winced, stumbled inside, and had a full-blown panic attack in front of the cheese. It wasn't so much the memory of what she did, it was all of them, and all the things they did. I couldn't figure out what it was that made me so weak. Everything seemed too close to my skin or too far away. I was outside my body watching myself grabbing as much cheese off the shelves as I could. Filling my coat pockets with big blocks of cheddar, shoving bags of grated mozzarella up my shirt and down my pants. It was everywhere, stuffed inside my trouser legs and packed into the arms of my long black thief coat. I cleared that fridge of anything remotely cheese-related. The security camera was pointed right at me. I knew the staff were watching, I didn't care, it felt like the right thing to do. By the time the manager and his assistant came over I was carrying *so much cheese*, they just grabbed each other, laughing and wheezing. They said I had to pay, especially since some of it was down my pants. When I emptied my pockets they escorted me out of the building and told me to never ever come back do you hear me you weird fucking cheese boy. Thankfully, Karen's daughter was gone. The pavement was littered with pink, lipstick-stained butts. She even left a cigarette on the window ledge, still burning despite the wind and rain. God knows I was poor enough and desperate enough to pick it up and finish it. Yeah I sucked it right down to the soggy butt, thinking 'Oh, fuck you... You fucking seagull...' In the top floor window of the new flats opposite the derelict bakery, a woman and her baby waved at me. I recognised them. It looked like they were underwater. When I waved back, she shut the curtains and turned out the lights. Suddenly two men came sprinting from behind the dodgy pizza place as a posh white car exploded. I watched it burn until the police arrived, and when they pulled over to the piss-soaked kerb and asked me what I saw I told them

everything.

## *Beavis & Butthead*

I heard our neighbours fucking today.
The bedroom window was open
so I stuck my head out, sniffing
the summer air for rain.
The lonely old fella next door
was just standing there, spellbound
on that gorgeous lawn, his mouth
hanging off the widowed bone
like my dreams about the future.
There's nothing I can do for him.
When he saw me, I said 'Huh-huh-huh'
& he did a dance, laughing 'He-he-he'
His name is also Bobby & that's okay.
It's nice to have two weird Bobbys.

## *Sticky Legs*

What kind of hell planet is this? My best friend's father loves Death Valley so much. He goes there *all the time.* Beyond the bedroom doorway desperate souls gasp for cool air like cattle on the streets of millions of years. There's always a weapon waiting somewhere soaking up the bloody moonlight. You can't sleep without a fan. You can't listen to the witching hour voices no matter what. They want to tell you all about your life in pictures so big they make happy memories look like soggy acid tabs. It's like a hot therapist's waiting room in this house. Our feet get stuck in the creaky parts of the floor like we're making a game of it, sharing space with demonic wizards full of cobwebs and fog and the rich stink of burning.

## *This Poem Will Make You Rich*

*Yum Yum Yum*

is the sound

graveyards make

when you're asleep.

## *I'm Going Over the Fence*

Depression is a bit like Tom Hanks
in my favourite scene from The 'Burbs
when Ray goes off the fucking rails
rummaging around in his pants
until he pulls a dead man's hairpiece
out of the right leg of his blue shorts
and starts manically finger-banging it
while Bruce Dern wrinkles his nose:
'You had that in your trousers *all day*?'

## *Ramble On*

I didn't laugh when she told me
her dad was attacked
by a herd of cows.

That must've been really scary.

Cows don't give a fuck.

## *Three Months Sober (and it's almost Halloween)*

The guy next-door thinks he's such a hero for being lonely. When a frightened woman screams for help on our street, he says it's silly what people do for attention. Sometimes I kneel with them in the road and they tell me what hurts as his face floats against the dark glass like a hungry fish. Most recently, I spoke with a woman who told me she used to be a nun. She was sitting under spectral halogen street light surrounded by torn bags full of clothes spilling out like swollen tongues. When the guy next-door came out to check on us, she waved at him and said, 'You must be a very nice man...' he just folded his arms, sniffing the wind for booze. I remember that spreading pool of piss, how it looked as if the ground was opening up beneath her but somehow I managed to make her laugh. After the ambulance took her away my neighbour said helping people like that is the worst thing you can do because they always come back begging to be your friend. He doesn't know that I have been that woman. That I could be that woman for him. Or he could be that woman for me. You can tell he's got money because his garden is stunning with a white dog and fairy lights and spinning metal sculptures. The way he has utilised such limited space kills me every time I go to my daughter's bedroom window and stare straight down. It has this magic atmosphere, like that secret corner at a festival where there's a pretty couch and maybe some water and someone you love is convinced you're never going to die. Looking at my neighbour's garden makes me want to get fucked up in the best possible way. It makes me want to get fucked up in the worst possible way. It makes me want to never have been so fucked up in the first place. He thinks he's such a hero, keeping his shit to himself. His name is also Bob. It's weird: I hate being called Bob but when I talk to myself I say, 'Fucking Hell, Bob.' Of course they come back, they're *supposed* to come back. We are nourished by the haunted. We live in return.

# *Skin Past Bone*

You're probably wondering why there's a hunting knife stuck in the wall above my baby brother's head. I know how it looks, and I agree. It's completely fucked. Can you see the way the stainless steel blade reflects badly on me? Gasping in the corner, tilted like a vandalised headstone. Doesn't seem real, does it? The mind-blowing odds. This situation. That bone-chilling fluke, an inch above his golden hair. I don't know how long we have been alone here. Our mom has three jobs (that I know about). She works in a doll parts factory during the week. Sometimes she brings me the heads. I melt them like marshmallows on a stick in the garden, their blonde hair fizzing under her candy pink lighter. It's Saturday today, so she's either scrubbing toilets in The Fighting Cocks or doing a shift in the dodgy betting shop on Grubb Street. The manager of the bookies is a greasy pig man called Jared. He reminds me of the raincoat goblin who licks the toilet doors in our rundown shopping centre. Jared only employs women, and he has this trick he likes to play on his employees. Whenever someone's long shot horse comes in, and they win so much it almost puts him out of business, Jared takes a shotgun into his smoky office and barricades the door with his desk. His fraught employees know he has a gun in there. My mom begs, screams, shakes uncontrollably. Everyone shouting, 'Don't do it, Jared!' Punching and kicking the door. Will he? Won't he? *Hilarious*. Meanwhile my baby brother is clapping and dribbling on the carpet, oblivious to what just happened. He doesn't know anything, except that he loves me. It's a miracle how close it came. Children only giggle this way for such a short time, it hurts to think about. It smells like my brother's nappy is full. I was only goofing around, bored like you wouldn't believe, starved of stimulation. The week-old birthday balloons are starting to sag. A cold breeze flickers in through the back door, making them nod to each other like sad old managers on the armchair nobody uses. Look at them leaking knackered breath, taunting me, begging to be popped. Whoa! I must have been holding it wrong. When I throw it, the flat side of the knife wallops off the red balloon like the second coming of Christ, zipping over my right shoulder into the wall above my darling brother's head. Holy piss! An inch closer and my brother would be dead. His small face crashes through my brain like a 1950s advert for dark red soap. Blinded, impaled, scarred for the rest our lives. Another doll head perishing before my soulless eyes. How would I explain? *Oh, you know, I was throwing knives at some balloons and the knife bounced off and maimed slash killed my baby brother?* Fuck no, you can't live with something like that. I would have to join him, using the same bastard knife. Open my throat like a nasty leather handbag. Even if he was injured - just a nick or a scratch - I wouldn't be able to live with myself. Look at that shot though! You can't tell me that's not a sign. I'm pretty sure our house is possessed by evil spirits. I'm always haunted when I'm alone. Isn't everybody? Jamie, the weird boy from three doors down, told me there's a demon for everything. He's not like the dicks who get picked on for being middle class and smart. Jamie is dirt poor with bad hygiene and his attitude stinks. We used to camp out in my garden so we could smoke the cigarettes we stole from our parents. One night as we lay on the grass looking at the stars Jamie told me girls don't do it for him, boys either, and he can only get rock hard when he thinks about horses and dogs. He swigged from a stolen bottle of rum until his eyes started to bubble and his voice went all sticky. He told me his mom found a dirty film called Animal Farm under his bed and his old man hit the roof and told him he couldn't have a dog. Ever. No pets for mister horse cock. He said there was a better chance of Jamie's grandparents clawing out of their cheap graves to crawl home and forgive him for being a piece of shit son than there was of buying a puppy. Jamie wiped thick gooey snot along his baggy sleeve. Then he jumped on top of me and tried to stick his thumb up my ass. I can almost see him hanging from that rope in a few years, skin past bone, neon vomit down his wife-beater. One night I heard a noise and, freaking myself out, went to investigate. It was just my dad, home early from the pub. 'Hahaha! You thought I was a ghost didn't you!' He giggled until he had one of his coughing fits. 'You would love… a good ghost… wouldn't you!' I've always been a broken sleeper. Ducky is driving me crazy. We walk all day in the rain and cheat on our partners with each other. But my cousin wouldn't break my jaw, even when the boys set it up, clearing a space at the heart of the abandoned garages. We are like brothers. The pain we have witnessed will last forever. Ducky was his first love. I'm not sure what she wants. Whenever we skip school and get bored of exploring the derelict carpet factory, I pretend to be asleep on the dirty mattress near the metal stairs. Once she's convinced I'm passed out I watch her through half-closed eyelids. Ducky can never tell in the dark. Lately she's been taking a pair of scissors out of her rucksack and holding them like a ceremonial knife. She stands over me with dark green hair in front of her face, whispering curses, working up the courage to stab me, as moonlight pours through the broken windows like non-toxic glue. I regret every makeshift ouija board, our seance in the ruins, summoning the queens of hell together. There's no way I can predict how many times things like this are gonna happen in my life, how hard the invisible force that protects me is going to have to work to keep me safe. Who pays them? Our guardian angels. Do we pay for their divine protection? After all is said and done, are we their dreadful prize? I go into the garden and hide the knife behind my dad's new tool shed, grinning like a brainwashed cult. Back in the house, my brother is giggling, he loves me more than anything. He calls me *Blob* and it makes me so fucking mad. Then it really hits me. I could have killed him. My family's golden child. A gift in the radiated aftermath of a young woman's cancer. Now I'm kneeling in the kitchen, listening to the busted fridge. Every five seconds it makes a deep mooing sound. My mom doesn't mind, but it drives the old man nuts. Maybe the heart is wearing out or something. I don't know much about fridges. It moos and moos. And I moo, too. I say *Oh my god… Moo moo moo.* My dad will be back from the pub soon. We haven't been getting along too well lately. I broke into our neighbour's greenhouse, fucked up their cactuses, and got involved in a burglary. My parents take turns slapping my face. It's almost cartoonish, like bad Kung Fu acting. I'm usually drunk and high. My mum smacks the hardest, by a long shot. Perhaps she hits me so hard that by the time it's my dad's turn to tap in, my face has already been numbed, or stings too much to register anything new. He doesn't seem to put any welly into his slaps at all. I don't know. Maybe it's the drugs. With some families you know love is there but you can't actually see it or feel it. They don't know how to say the word avalanche until it's too late and one of us is freezing to death. People round here measure love in terms of how much better off you have it than someone who is truly suffering. They say things like, *You kids don't know you're born!* and *Oh come on, it can't be as bad as Liam - his crazy mother wanted a girl. Bitch tried to drown that boy the first chance she got.* I hope my brother won't remember what happened. He will grow into a kind-hearted, hardworking man. We will send each other a message every New Year's Eve at midnight with soppy promises to see more of each other. Then we will spend the rest of the year like strangers again. I was twelve when he was born. One night, while I was babysitting, he completely vanished. I mean his cot was empty. It was like that scene with the goblins from the movie Labyrinth starring David Bowie's crotch. I frantically searched the house and the garden, crying, mad with fear. Then I went back into his room and looked in his cot again and there he was, fast asleep. What was happening to me? I ate six king size Mars bars and threw up in the dog basket under the stairs. Last weekend my parents rented a film called Shallow Grave (1994). I watched it in the dark. I was wearing my favourite sailor pyjamas. They called around midnight to ask if everything was okay. 'Mom, this film is really disturbing! Three friends found their room-mate dead in bed with a huge amount of cash beside him. They buried his body in the woods after chopping his hands and feet off!' The pub sounded packed that night. Pool balls hitting each other like cartoon skulls, twisted laughter, people stamping their feet. I heard my mom turn to my dad: 'It's Bobby... I said it's your son! He says the film's *disturbing!* Hahahahaha.' Maybe they thought I was happy. My brother was screaming and I begged them to hurry as the rain struck my window like rapid, angry dots on my teacher's blackboard. They always buy me some chow mein from the Chinese takeaway on their way home. My dad likes to pretend he got them from a graveyard. 'Here's yer creepy worms!' He really gets a kick out of that. It takes forever for their headlights to fill up the silky blue curtains. When my brother was three months old I remember sitting on the sofa, cradling him in my arms as he cried his ass off. His face was purple. He sounded like an injured goat. My parents were late. It was past midnight. I didn't know how to look after a baby. I was a maniac, traumatised, obsessed with alternate realities, where the monsters were love. Or a version of love I could comprehend. My brother's wailing reached such a pitch that I bit him on his leg. I could have shaken him, tossed him around, rattled his brains out, but

I didn't. Now, that frightened the life out of me - the bite and the scary thoughts I had afterwards. I always found another way to add to the weight of my shame. Our bodies remember. The first time I heard the word *degloved* was when my uncle described an accident at work. Someone's leg slipped through the gap between the loading bay and the lorry, stripping the skin clean off their leg. Now I've come to believe that time itself has been degloved, the mutilated flesh of history dripping blood all over us, the gory past, oozing pus and chunder. I'm sorry, that's gross I know. I hate to say it, but that's the way I feel. This time, that time, all the time. Horrifying. Carved off the bone. I can't tell gore from nostalgia, pain from retro-mania. Tomorrow is just another disposable mask. I was obsessed with the rain lamp at my grandparents' house. It had a metallic Venus inside, surrounded by shiny plastic foliage. It worked by using a pump that ran oil over several strands of taut fishing line to create a slow motion effect that resembled rain. My dad bought the lamp for my grandmother. He remembers carrying it through the snow on Christmas Eve, stoned out of his mind, shielding it with his black leather jacket in case he tripped on a patch of ice. He said that lamp cost him a month's wages. Sometimes I think about asking his estranged brother to convert his old family videos into a digital file so that my old man can hear his mother's voice again. We forget because our minds are so noisy. Sometimes it sends our most precious impressions to the trash. Would that be a nice thing to do? Or would a lifetime of repressed emotion come crashing out of his chest like a great white shark? In the dream we were standing around their rain lamp, my grandparents and I, and all around us was this endless, growling darkness and the only light was the lamp, and we were standing over it as if it was the last hope at the end of all things. I was looking up at them, hoping they would speak, because they never spoke. For some reason their relationship, the way they communicated with each other, had been frozen in a decades-long silence. No one knows why. I'm guessing my grandad did a bad thing. He was in the war. He was a postman. He went completely mad without her. I was begging them to say something about the rain lamp being the last light of the world. Teach me how to work it. They were smiling with large eyes full of wonder. They opened and closed their mouths like hungry turtles, sighing so hard my flesh rippled. Then the lamp went out. My family had gone out for the day, so I must have been alone in the house when it happened. I only heard the doorbell because I was blowing dust off a secondhand copy of Nevermind on vinyl. I ran downstairs to open the door, praying it wasn't the police. There had been two officers watching the house. They couldn't arrest me because I was under sixteen, which means there has to be a guardian present. The pigs knocked at regular intervals to make sure I wasn't trying to escape over the garden fence. I was involved in what the law considers a "dwelling burglary". A few lads from the estate robbed one of my neighbours and sold the stuff to an outlaw biker for nothing but snack money. They didn't know what they had. Easily £20,000 worth of heirlooms, gold sovereigns, diamond necklace, a sweet old woman's engagement ring. All of it traded in for munchies. For some reason they thought I was the mastermind, when in fact I was the dirty grass. In the end, the boys got copies of my statement. 'It was like reading a fucking novel!' Keith cackled, closing the door. Pinhead, poker-faced as always, nodded at a signal from Keith, snapped open the tool box and caressed a rusty hammer. Of course it wasn't the police knocking my door. The sound was too gentle. I opened it to find some nice fella with a package for my dad. He was handsome and he had this comforting energy that confused me. I took the box and thanked him. When he smiled it was like gazing into the reflection of red clouds on clear water. I felt like a child's paper boat covered with glitter and sequins, drifting into him, leaning to one side and then leaning to the other until I started to sink. My dad called me names when I was small. It was banter, I know that now, but I'm not sure he knew that at the time. Maybe no one showed him how to be a father. He would wiggle his index finger and call me a faggot whenever I got upset. I cried a lot. But one day, shopping in the supermarket with my mom, I saw it. My nickname staring back at me from inside a frosted Iceland freezer. The penny dropped. Faggots! Bright yellow packages with images of steaming balls of meat. So that's what I was. I stared at myself in the tall mirror hanging on the back of my bedroom door. Faggot. My long hair was ridiculous. Faggot. Thick, coppery, curling at the ends. Faggot. I took off my clothes and threw them on the bed. My body was pale and skinny. Covered with chicken pox scars. Nothing manly about it. Was I a girl? What else could it be? How else could I have felt such overwhelming attraction to that delivery man? I examined the seam along my scrotum. I used to think it was evidence that I was born a female, and that some mad doctors manufactured my penis as a joke. I started punching myself in the head, over and over, slapping my face and yanking my hair, raking my scarred chest with my fingernails. I thumped myself in the balls so hard I doubled over on the floor, shrieking with manic laughter, all grief and spit and tears, wiggling my pink faggot fingers until what is forbidden began to melt and vanish into the piss-stained carpet. Here are my favourite knife superstitions: A dropped knife means a crooked man will visit. Eating from a knife makes you *angry like a dog*. It's bad luck to say the word knife when you're at sea. Place a knife under the bed during childbirth to ease the pain of labor. You should always cut bread with a knife rather than breaking it with your hands - it's said that your life will be broken otherwise. If you play with knives the angels will run away from you. Some knife throwing acts involve a trick in which the thrower palms the knife as they pretend to throw it, and a knife springs out from the target, giving the illusion of perfect aim. I wish that is what happened. In an alternate universe, a fourteen year old version of me murdered his baby brother. In another, he didn't play with knives at all. Some say it's the parents who are to blame for the rot inside their offspring. Do you think that's true? My image is so confusing. The yearning for makeup and certainty. A body at odds with itself, becoming older, softer, out of focus. Damn brother, I'm afraid there's been a terrible accident. They left me. They left me with you. They left us alone. Time is about to speed up something shocking. Forgive them for me, will you?

## *Midnight Snack*

You're not creeping downstairs
for a slimy piece of chicken
and a secret cry in the fridge.
Not this time, pal. It's too late.
You're staying right here in bed
with ear worms and tinnitus.
Wicked visions. A mountain
of doll heads in the dark.
Consider this your punishment
for relapse on a bastard scale.
No one cares if you can't sleep
and your mother's face appears
like black mould on the ceiling.
Everyone struggles, you know?
We're all trying to make sense.
If you make it through the night
the universe will be so impressed.
It might send you a clean day.
Remember those? Sweet dreams.

## *Come Down (Three Bad Dreams)*

The sausage looked so lonely in the chip shop window. I had to buy it. But I made a mistake. The sausage was evil. As soon as I unwrapped the soggy paper I knew it was a diabolical purchase. I just get that spooky feeling about stuff sometimes. Like our German room-mate's well-worn Birkenstocks. Bastard things in the world. I carefully placed the greasy sausage onto a clean plate that was still wet from the dishwasher. It looked fine. It smelled fine. I threw it away and left the room. That's when it spoke to me, with a voice like a chewed-up dog toy squeaking in the depths of the kitchen bin. Do you want to know what it said? No, of course you don't. No one wants to hear what an evil sausage has to say. I did find, however, if you pay attention to such phenomena, you can access the truth. You sense the wickedness in your surroundings and the cruelty in your neighbours. At least that's what I thought, until Sock Head told me they arrested Taylor: 'Why do you think he always stayed with friends who have small children...' I threw up stringy yellow by the side of the road, worrying about everyone I know. Were they evil? I couldn't tell any more. That's when I walked by the chip shop and saw that godforsaken sausage. I was vulnerable, you see. The thought of carrying a device that connects us to more human suffering than the brain can possibly process suddenly appeared to me as a severed head floating through an empty shopping mall. I was feeling guilty for neglecting my family. My poor nan has been waiting months for me to visit. She lives two streets away from the chip shop in a small flat full of fake cats curled up in cute little baskets. She used to paint the same ugly horse over and over again. Never told us its name. Maybe I'll go see her tomorrow. I need more information about the beast she sees creeping out of the asphalt. It's my favourite story. Nan loves telling that one, her soft hands mauling the air as she rises out of her rocker, showcasing the scene with effortless B-movie grace.

I was smoking weed through a skull-shaped glow in the dark bong under my desk in the garage when I saw Frank's tattooed legs stagger up the sunlit driveway and collapse in my chair. He looked haunted. Things must be really bad for Frank to come here. Even when we were friends we rarely saw each other. I pretended to be a groaning zombie, rising with a guttural moan from behind my cluttered desk, which made him nervous. 'How are you?' I asked, searching for a lighter. *'How are you?'* He mimicked, folding his arms. I gently raked my fingers across the brick wall, picturing sparks. The ice cream van went by, cranking its creepy old stories. Maybe it was a Sunday because everything was sad and still and I could hear the bells. I was about to apologise when Frank said, 'I can't stop watching horrible things. It's like they've built a nest inside my brain and now the wires are tangled.' I think he was talking about porn, but he might have been talking about the news. 'Does this mean you're angry with God?' I was being mischievous. I've never met anyone who believes in God the way Frank believes in God. I took my hat off because I wanted to show him how much hair I'm losing. 'Remember when we were kids?' I said. *'Remember when we were kids?'* he repeated. Frank tried to remove his enormous black shirt, which seemed to grow bigger the more he struggled. I don't know if he expected me to help. It was too hot to expect anything. Next thing I know, both of us are trapped inside his biblical shirt as it swallowed my garage and covered the house. 'I'm sorry, are you lost?' I shouted, into Frank's billowing blackness. 'Because I've done worse things than being queer…'

I was racing through the park in a stolen wheelchair on the hottest day of the year when I saw your chronic pain on the playing field, throwing tennis balls for neighbourhood dogs. It had a seemingly endless supply, which it plucked from what looked like a tall man's body bag. I was disgusted with myself for using again. My spit was thick and sticky from eating too many oranges. A little girl was flying a kite that wasn't actually a kite it was a bad-tempered doctor biting the clouds. A gang of shirtless boys armed with axes and hammers were merrily destroying the new playground. I thought I saw my parents buried waist deep in the sandpit, shrieking like seagulls. I emptied a bottle of water over my head, hoping it would bring me closer to you. When that didn't work I gathered broken glass from the forgotten basketball court and put the pieces in my mouth. Late afternoon sun dripped like morphine through the shivering trees. Your pain was so impressive even the ice cream man was crying.

## Resurrection Mary

This photo was taken at 15:09 pm, December 24th, 2019. The last time I went to visit Mary. At the time of writing it's January 23rd, 2021. It's snowing. The nights are endless guilt and silence. Eerie streets and sirens. Mary's flat is only a ten minute walk from here. You can probably see it from my bedroom window.

That's Mary's handwriting on the inside of her front door. This door was her diary, notebook and calendar. I suppose she was more likely to remember these events since she spent a lot of time behind that door, listening for killers she heard lurking in the communal hallway.

- 

A concerned nurse wrote: *Do not open for anyone except ambulance, police or family!* In red marker above the door handle. There was also a small poem for Baby Jesus above the peep hole. I took a photo of her cute poem but I must have deleted it.

- 

Mary had a nightmare neighbour. His name was Paul. He lived upstairs. Paul would bug her for teabags or spare change, but mostly he wanted to use her landline to call his dealer. I was having tea with Mary one day when Paul conned his way in. He looked like a haunted bottle of milk. His eyes practically leapt out of his skull when he saw me sitting on the sofa. He expected Mary to be alone. 'Sorry, sweetheart!' He sighed, slapping the doorframe. 'I just remembered I left the gas on.'

- 

Paul died from an overdose a week later. Mary found him in the corridor, slumped against the electric meter. 'He looked like a sleeping child,' she sighed. 'Picasso. Blue Period.'

- 

Those dots, scattered across the surface of the door in the photo, mark the places where Mary's pen veered off. I'm fascinated by its erratic constellation. Frightened, even. It's like an exploded thought. A bad idea.

•

It's the anniversary of Mary's aneurysm. She was having her eyes tested twenty years ago when the optician told her to go to the hospital immediately. They caught it in time. Since then, her hand shakes uncontrollably. She drinks tea through a straw on the table because she can't hold the cup. Mary would make the tea extremely hot, it was a way of prolonging social contact. Steam slicing through a blade of sunlight falling through the curtains. Another story? Oh, go on! Smiling as you burn your lips.

•

I missed out on building my daughter's first snowman with her. This is the kind of thing that eats me up inside. She must have been two years old. I had the flu. I was weak, tripping nuts with a high fever. My ex took our daughter to my parents' garden where the snow was untouched. I stayed in bed watching Frasier. I liked it when Frasier and Niles spoke French in front of Eddie the dog because they didn't want Eddie to know what they were saying.

•

Mary always tried to sneak money into my hand, like a spy with secret codes that might win the war. She did this even if no one was around to scold her for her generosity. The older I got the more I protested. But she wouldn't take no for an answer. Money was a secret thing. She grew up hiding it. The tremor in her hand made this sweet transaction more difficult, even comical. We laughed and laughed! I'm a terrible grandson.

•

Clammed up folks, am I right? Folded notes instead of hugs. Pound coins for kisses. Did I only love Mary for my pocket money? I'm grateful, don't get me wrong. Some people don't get love or Christmas gifts. I wanted someone to listen. Instead, I got a bunch of Action Man dolls with muscles I found confusing. When I was assaulted, I wish I could have told them that was the reason I was so screwed up. I would've happily traded all the toys in the world to be able to say, 'Mom, I was assaulted by my friend Terry. He used the old man's knife. His knob looked like a lonely pirate.

•

If we become ghosts, well, there must be a ghost jumping around inside of you right now. A ghost that's patiently waiting for the end of pain and bodies when, according to Mary, the real show begins, you lucky phantoms!

•

Did I tell you about the time Mary won the lottery? Well, her numbers came in (the ones she used every week) but Mary forgot to go to the shop and buy the ticket. My dad wouldn't speak to her for weeks. Imagine how different our lives would've been? My God, the therapy!

∙

Mary used to buy and sell antique dolls and toys. She would sell a piece for next to nothing and then discover, a few years later, it was worth a small fortune. At my estimation - and if her stories are true - Mary lost millions over the years, but she always had a sense of humour about it.

∙

What strikes me about this photo is how long it would've taken Mary to write my name. It looks as if there was an earthquake that day. I imagine her standing there, fighting the failed currents of her brain, tongue sticking out in concentration. See the way the letters seem to strangle themselves? How that capital T resembles a slipshod crucifixion? It reminds me of the profane, witchy messages that some outpatients left all over the bus stop.

∙

I didn't go to see Mary that Tuesday at 8 pm. Did I even intend to visit? I'm not sure. That was a long time ago. Before the pandemic. Anything was possible. We took so much for granted. Will I ever stop disappointing the people who love me? Close friends and fellow poets. My own flesh and blood.

•

That would've been the last time I saw her. When she was still Mary. The Mary that I remember. Not the one who I couldn't face any more because the stories she told got darker. Spiteful. Increasingly paranoid. Not the one who, right now, is lying on a bed in the hospital corridor because the wards are overrun with coronavirus. She might die. And I know this is going to sound awful but it feels like she already did.

•

Maybe a part of my unravelling mind already erased Mary's love. Buried her. Forgot about her. Perhaps the meds have made me colder, disconnected. It's a common side effect and quite fucking welcome to be honest.

•

I love the sound snow makes when it's too heavy for the branches. When it falls onto the fluffy lawn like muffled coughs in the attic, or bags of meds slumping off the backseat of a lonely night bus.

•

Mary's mental illness frightened me, okay? I've been around seriously unstable characters all my life. Proper horror movie shit. And then there's Mothman, Mary's evil ex-husband. The one my family doesn't want us to talk about.

•

I'm trying to make myself cry. I'm thinking about Mary in that bleak hospital corridor, scared, alone, hallucinating, missing me. But nothing happens. I used to cry ten times a day before I started taking Sertraline. 'Boohoo!' – Breaking News. Come on, cry! If you don't cry how do you know you can love? I want to cry because I'm becoming increasingly frightened of my detachment. My eyes are too dry. It's like trying to break a fresh apple with my numb, anxious hands.

•

Mary was digging in her garden when she was a child. She found a wooden box with a ginger ponytail inside. The way she explained it, it was as if she found the soul of a girl who was forced to marry a spooky politician on her sixteenth birthday. Mary said she burned the ponytail in the kitchen sink using her mother's cooking matches. That week, rising flood water breached the family home. Neighbours started getting sick. Her brother died. Then her cousin died. The milkman's house burned down. But Mary was beautiful and that, she said, was the main thing.

•

I had beans for breakfast and I can't stop farting. Some of them feel wet and they burn. I should take a shower. It might even relax me. We just found out Mary tested negative for coronavirus, again. It must be something else. Something she caught in the care home. Mary's daughter hasn't been able to physically touch her for almost a year. She might never touch her again. They stare at each other through the care home window. Do you think people will be kinder to each other after the pandemic or will we go back to business as usual? Gives me chills just thinking about it.

•

*Brrr...* Someone just walked over my grave.

•

'You know that ornament you bought Mary for Christmas? Oh shut up, you do! That lovely little bird? Yes! Well, she asked for it. Your uncle took it to her. It makes her feel closer to you. Mary holds your bird for comfort.'

•

I wish I could call her. We used to chat for hours on the phone. Mary's stories from her days as a mental health nurse are literally insane. As beautiful as they are terrifying. But even if I could call her, I'd need to explain everything. I'd need her to explain everything. I don't think she's up to that. I mean, who is?

•

In my earliest memory of Mary I have chicken pox. My uncle holds me down on the floor and farts on my back. It feels like beef gravy thunder. Mary is scraping the jelly from the bottom of a can of cat food then licking the spoon. In the fenced off area at the bottom the garden, a power unit growls with a sign that reads: KEEP OUT! DANGER OF DEATH! with one of those stick figure pictures of Saul's conversion on the road to Damascus.

•

Do I want her forgiveness? I'm not so sure. I always want forgiveness, it's my biggest flaw. I guess if I could just tell Mary that I would never have made it this far as an artist without her support. Without her money. Fuck. Is art all I care about? Is that such a bad thing? Maybe it is. She loved talking about art with me, even though Mary wasn't educated or knowledgeable, art still interested her. She listened very patiently when I told her about the life of Francis Bacon. Mary loved anything with meat. She really believed in me, you know?

•

I'm talking as if she's already gone, like she isn't in that hospital corridor right now, burning under a white sheet, running her fingers over an ornament I honestly don't remember buying.

•

Mary bred Siamese cats when I was a kid. I hated them. I was cruel. The smell of piss and cat food. Her smell forever. The way she wandered through the house, pining for a lover called Jimmy the Shoe. People travelled from all over to buy one of Mary's Siamese cats. Her main girl, Crystal, ended up being torn apart by a neighbour's Alsatian. She didn't want any more cats after that. Her affection for animals disappeared. It's not that she disliked them, they just became invisible. The natural world held no value. Even the sea was out.

•

It's strange when someone you think you know becomes associated with a certain thing - like cocaine or heavy drinking - and when that thing has gone, their real personality rises to the surface. And it's not always good. If you think about it, even the people we love most could change at any moment. They could wake up one day and silently walk out the door and never come back.

•

Before she retired, Mary worked as a mental health nurse for twenty years. The ward was known locally as D Block. I know a lot of people who were sectioned there. Mary looked after them. They really loved her. She would comb their hair and dance with them at Christmas parties. Mary was also privy to unbelievable levels of human suffering. Sometimes we would sit in a cafe in the centre of town, eating bacon sandwiches, and she would point at a man or a woman walking by, telling me about their tragic lives. Her stories profoundly shaped the way I think about the world.

•

Mothman shifts from scene to scene like a hotel creep's binoculars. Mary didn't know about his past. No one did (apart from his victims). Mothman would break Mary's nose and leave the country for a while. Sometimes she would get a phone call from Paris, Malta or Germany. 'Guess where I am? Go on, guess!' After the divorce, Mary could still hear Mothman growling down the faulty line. Hell bound, praying for answers.

•

Lockdown dream about a nasty old cake with gruesome cherries mangled in the icing. Mothman's cake. He made it for us. There must be a small radio inside. Industrial blues. A young girl screaming. Antique dolls rolling their glassy eyes as Mary grabs a fistful of cake. She wants me to try it first, in case it's poisoned. I open my mouth as wide as possible.

•

I want to be vulnerable

the way those kids

were vulnerable

but only in my work.

•

When Mothman called her from prison, Mary would giggle and take the phone behind the crushed velvet curtains. Mary would pretend it was a nice young man selling windows, life insurance, burial plots. She would say things like, 'Oh yes, I definitely need one of those.' and *whispering* 'Thank you for the gorgeous roses!'

•

I want her to confess, forgive me, be innocent.

Her laughter like… I can't.

His victims like… I'm sorry, I can't.

- 

D Block used to have a pond. It was near the creepy smoking shed behind the bushes. I used to watch the fish and think about my traumas. They were the whitest fish I've ever seen. I named them after English poets. They ate crusts from my sandwiches. When the pond froze over in winter I would worry about the fish so much it gave me a rash.

- 

When Mary had an aneurysm, her face was peeled off by a surgeon who stitched it back all wrong. Her loose skin sagged under one green eye. Her shaved head tracked with oozing staples. As a frightened boy, I couldn't look at her. Our family's bloodshot moneybags. Giving me money. Giving me so much of her money. I never paid her back.

- 

Scrapbook mother of misfits and runaways, screaming because the man next door bangs his cane on the wall, yelling that he knows.

- 

Mary considered legal action against the local paper for printing her name in Mothman's story. For saying that she will stand by him. How could she have known? It happened forty years ago. Mary was still married to grandad then. She was too busy throwing her daughter's clothes out the bedroom window as lightning flashed in her eyes.

•

Lockdown nightmare: It was Mother's Day times a million and a dog called Sally saved my ass. Sally was magic and all she wanted to talk about was Auschwitz, America, Antarctica. Schools all across the world were filling with blood. I found out my childhood friends didn't exist. Doctors setting themselves on fire in the streets like Tibetan monks.

•

When Mary moved to a care home she didn't want to kill her neighbours anymore. She didn't hide in the shadows of assisted living, whispering to a butcher's knife and staring into blackness like a promenade clairvoyant. She couldn't take anything with her. Her furniture was either sold or given away. I called dibs on the cutlery. Didn't want the TV. Said no to the world's saddest bed. But her old front door? That is something else. Her zigzag scrawl like a seance in black marker, debunked above the misty spy hole. You know me well enough to believe I want that lonely door! Would you pay the council to release it, free it from the hinges and deliver it from evil for me, please? I'll keep it in the garden and hammer on it like the police in the rain when I'm mad.

•

Soft scoop Mary jangles in the distance like an urban legend, loving me. Her posh coat and scarves vanishing and reappearing on buses and trains. Charity shops and snooty cafes. She stopped going out because the people who occupied her favourite spaces became demons to her. Pointing, hissing to each other: That's Mothman's wife! Of course she knew!

•

I tipped the Domino's delivery driver a handful of notes. I didn't mean to give him so much. It was a mistake. I was distracted by the moon. He kept saying, 'Wow, are you sure?' His gratitude made me depressed. It's still snowing and the road is frozen. I watched him tread carefully to his car. For some reason I waved as he reversed off the drive. He waved back, laughing, flashing the money which made me want to kill myself. His tyres skidding and all kinds of fucked up stars.

•

Mary asked us if they talked about her on the internet, as if Mothman was an unusual thing! She saw shadow people lurking in the bushes outside her window, their sharp-toothed mouths dripping with rotten egg yolks. They became her jailers. They taught her how to barricade the door, turn off all the lights and listen as the darkness from all corners told her everything.

•

Mary's favourite favourite place to hide was Venice. After the divorce - flush with half that bastard's money - Venice became her second home. She was looked after there. A safe place that suited her middle class persona. A chance to escape the past. No one knew anything apart from her name and that her purse was seemingly bottomless. She wanted to take me there, since I've never left the UK. She wanted to show me Peggy Guggenheim's grave. The graves of Peggy's dogs, her beloved babies. Pretending to be a rich old lady. Who knows, I might have had a good time. I doubt it. Mothman cast a dark shadow over her. A stain. For some reason I was the only one who could see it.

•

I'm writing this to keep her alive
to keep her alive to keep her alive
I'm writing this to keep her alive
because if Mary reads this I'm dead.

•

Mother will never forgive me. Mary's family will never forgive me. But I can't stop. I'm not supposed to stop. You're not supposed to walk away from a ritual until you've closed all the doors.

•

I was in my early twenties when I went to an art gallery for the first time. Tate Modern in London. They had a video installation by the American artist Paul McCarthy projected on three screens in a dark room. He was naked apart from a clown mask and boxing gloves. He was punching himself in the dick and smearing his body with what looked like faeces. I had to run outside for a cigarette. It really shook me up. In a good way. I couldn't keep still.

•

Mary lived in a lot of different houses when I was growing up, and in every house, above every fireplace, she would hang one of those sad clown paintings that used to be so popular. Her homes were always gloomy. Filled with secrets. Hidden money. The ghost of Bread Man, another long dead lover, stomping up and down the stairs in the middle of the night. Howling. The smell of burning toast.

- 

Mary has the best ghost stories. She has seen monsters, too. When she worked in D Block there was a phantom nurse from the forties who walked through walls and floated around corridors. They called her Bessie and she didn't have a face. Bessie was a bad omen. Her sightings often meant someone would die on the ward that night. Mary started leaving offerings to Bessie, in the hope of appeasing her spirit and helping her to move on. But Bessie was queen of the night and no amount of biscuits and flowers was going to change that.

- 

Before we knew what Mothman had done my family had suspicions. He would disappear for weeks at a time. Mary was happy to live in his house. He paid all the bills which meant her money was essentially her own. She could indulge her doll collecting without worrying about the cost. For a while, we thought Mothman must be involved with trafficking drugs. Perhaps that was the reason for his erratic moods. He spent hours in the bathroom. What was he doing in there? I remember when he bought a motorbike called a FireBlade. He raced it all over Europe and the Isle of Man until he was injured in a crash. Turns out he had another family. Another wife. They lived on a farm. Fuck, I hope they didn't have any kids.

•

Oh yeah! The monster in the pavement. Mary said she was walking through the park one summer evening after her shift when the pavement started to move like a conveyor belt and no matter how fast she walked, Mary wasn't going anywhere. The sky was fizzing television static and a monster came out of the ground and Mary told me it looked like the devil's liquid ballgown. The best way Mary could describe it was by making her hands look like claws and growling as she got up out of her chair with her face twisting in four different directions.

•

I hope Mary's family doesn't read this, but if they are they reading this, if you are Mary's family reading this, I need you to know I kept her alive. When I started writing this Mary was in the hospital we thought she was going to die. The nurse just called to say Mary is out of the hospital and on her way back to the care home. Who knows, maybe she'll survive long enough for me to clear my conscience. Is that what I want? Am I getting to know myself? Do you believe in the power of blood?

•

Mary used to say that I shouldn't worry about seeing my daughter so much. When Mary was a child she was lucky to receive the odd letter from her distant father. He was an electrician during the war. He was tall. He played chess. That's all I know. I couldn't seem to get her to understand I wanted to see my daughter more than anything. A lot of things fell into place when Mary told me that. A family lacking empathy, perhaps, roots in rotten soil.

•

Mary asked me to go into Mothman's attic to see if I could find anything valuable. This was before divorce proceedings had started. I don't know how old I was. When it comes to Mary, memory is twisted. She has that effect on me. In the same way my daughter makes me feel as though time is speeding up, Mary slows it down. She covers everything with dust.

•

The snow has turned to grey slush in the rain. A few patches of white are still holding out amongst the filth and the gutters are gurgling. Someone kicked the snowman apart, the one my ex came over to build with my daughter. I left them to it. Later, when my ex had gone and my daughter was in the bath, I went out to examine their snowman. I thought it would make me cry. Nothing. An echo of an echo of a torment long since dampened under its own layer of pharmaceutical snow. I consider trying to put their snowman back together. I get distracted by the colour of the moon. The older I get the brighter the moon seems to shine.

•

'She was beautiful when she was young.' That's what they tell me. Folk from the estate. I'm sure they mean well but I want to know what kind of person she was, the dreams she had. Hobbies. Stories that aren't about unusual men. What turned her into Mary?

•

I stood on a dining chair and pulled myself up through the entrance of Mothman's attic, careful to avoid the clumps of itchy fibreglass insulation, rolled out like yellowed gauze between the beams. I was hoping for more information about Mary. What she was to the world before being the Mary I knew and the woman in pub men's stories. The old lady who bugs the hell out of her daughter because there's some shit between them they can't reasonably explore. I was hoping to find evidence. Photos. I had to know where she came from. What misery brought the moths?

•

I'm squeezing my sad daughter's brain, worrying about my ex, her loser boyfriend, incompetent cops. Its pink maze bubbles in my fist, surprisingly cold. You can squeeze the granny out of it and it doesn't even come close to popping. It's one of those novelty stress relievers you find in strip mall gift shops. A stocking filler she had for Christmas. So soft!

•

My little girl is upset but she doesn't tell me why. It used to be simple. She dropped her favourite toy: I picked it up. She couldn't sleep: I warmed a cup of milk. I don't promise I can fix the world. That would be the wrong thing to say. I'm trying to build a space between us where she can tell me anything everything whatever hurts.

•

When we play Would you rather? My daughter asks me to choose between being rich or being popular. I've worn out dozens of stress balls over the years, especially those fleshy ones with spray-on smiley faces. My daughter's brain is like a giant American marshmallow, pummelled by divorce. She gets it from me, squeezing things. We've been through wine corks, healing crystals, balled up sheets of foil. All objects lose their power eventually. It's not as if we can take them with us when we leave. I said I would rather we change the question. I said I would rather we help each other. I said I promise you are safe here.

•

Now I'm holding my daughter's head. Kissing the top of it. Stroking her perfect skull with my nose. Her hair smells like old times and fresh court documents. I hope she'll understand when she's older. Her parents' classic horror. Our special effects.

•

According to this solicitor
court ordered drug tests
can be very expensive

she told us
that hair
is cheaper than blood.

•

The system is fucked

you know this

you know all sorts of things

*I love that about you!*

•

I've heard some poets say
they can't stand people
who write about parenthood,
as if their obsession
with shitty relationships
is so important.
We play along though, don't we?
Isn't that a fun expression:
They don't know that we
know they're lying...

•

Only kidding, you mean the world to me, you rascal!

•

Now my daughter wants her sad brain back. When she holds it against her cheek a tear falls onto the squishy surface and runs along the folds. She is grieving. We are all grieving. I don't ask if she would rather live with me or her mother. She is going to have to make that choice sooner or later. At some point we all run out of little things to squeeze.

•

I hope Mothman caught the virus.

I hope he died before he got the chance

to hurt anyone else. I suppose we'll never know.

•

It's January 31st, 2021. The snow has gone.

I don't miss Mary any more. It's been too long.

The truth sucks. But I love her and that's okay.
Love doesn't have to be straightforward.

I wrote this sequence in one week
as a middle finger to my perfectionism,
which has been in control for too long.

I couldn't finish anything.

I needed to get something out,
no matter how sloppy and disjointed.

I wanted to tell you about Mary.

I wanted to dive into the grey area and see
what kind of love exists inside
that glowing fog.

•

I found a box of receipts in Mothman's attic.
They belonged to Mary.
I recognised the dates and transactions.
Roast chicken dinners, two pots of tea,
fruit cake and diet cokes.
Every Thursday from 2003 to 2013.
The receipts were from
her favourite greasy spoon,
Hot Stuff, which was situated
near the town centre
above an expensive tailor and a hair salon
for salty old queens.
Mary would buy us lunch
and tell me stories about D Block.
I was a dysfunctional addict at the time
and lunch with Mary was one of
the few things I had to look forward to.

•

Mothman's attic was one of the most boring attics I've ever seen, and I've seen a lot of attics. I suppose my expectations for attics are pretty high. This one didn't even have cobwebs.

There were four neat rows of cardboard boxes, taped up and labelled. VHS tapes, tax records, motorcycle magazines. I couldn't cut the boxes open to have a look, Mothman might find out we had been snooping and give Mary hell.

You know that feeling you get when you're looking through dusty black holes in the attic and suddenly half an hour zips by because you tripped into the past and lost track of time?

Well that happened to me, when I found a tatty old brown envelope under all those Hot Stuff receipts.

•

The least we can do for our elderly relatives is try to be there at the end. Don't let them slip away alone or among strangers. Hold their hand. Tell them you love them. Sing a song. Say a soothing prayer. That's what I used to think, anyway. Of course, an ending can take a long time. It can last years. Do you have the stomach for that? Is there any other choice?

•

Being immature and completely ignorant of real responsibilities, I spent my twenties taking drugs and teaching myself to write and paint. Gathering material, picking up odd personalities the way some people collect vintage clothes. Back then, family was mostly the net I fell into from a great height. What mattered was the high, it was all I cared about. You could say they afforded me the luxury of getting as high as I could. Pain was something you ran from as fast as possible. I couldn't even look at it. I was an escape artist. I'm talking real bad, people always found me. I was an esape artist. Ha! Look at me now.

•

What was in
the brown envelope
I found in Mothman's attic
under all those Hot Stuff receipts?

•

I'm thinking about the damage

the harm my words have done to others

wondering if writing more poetry

is just going to make things worse.

•

But this isn't poetry.

•

This is wrong. I mean the picture, the memory of that sad clown painting, it doesn't make sense. The nightmarish figure was standing on a wooden box with blue smoke drifting out of his shoes, rising to veil his makeup with a blur.

I used to lie on my belly on Mary's sheepskin rug and watch the smoke curl out of the painting and around the lampshade. Sometimes it filled the room and I couldn't breathe. I had asthma attacks but no one would believe it was the clown smoke drifting out of the clown painting into my lungs my blood my clothes my hair.

But Mary believed.

Of course she believed.

She never doubted me for a second.

●

A heavily creased photo.

New Years Eve Party, D Block, 1982.

A message on the back said:

*Forgetting our problems tonight x x x*

## *Wackadoodle*

Crops are rotting all over the country
you can smell it on the breeze
like grandpa's gangrene cigar

I'm trying to turn into a horse
a dark one
yeah to hell with it

I need a family that understands
their boy transforms

I want a family that says Fuck me
she's a horse now

he used to be full
of Bobby bones
and Parker blood

who knows what else
is waiting out there

I can't promise the scarecrows
are gonna jump down
from their crosses
to save us from this one

but with a simple corkscrew
wire in the neck
they will look down
on our doomed wheat and oozing potatoes

their heads will shake
in the wind for you

they will yell *Goddamn*
and *Bless You All*

and the queer scarecrows
will touch themselves and cry.

# *Eight Lincolnshire Sausages*

Dear Jonathan, found in a fizzing puddle of puke, you were heavy for a short arse. I was your most sensitive coffin bearer and your outlaw biker friends hated my tearful eulogy. I was wearing an extra large coat to cover my tits because that's how soft I was back then. Three boxes of codeine washed down with a bottle of vodka because your wife caught you cheating? Because you couldn't afford to buy a gun? I used to mourn. I used to eat a thick wedge of sorry cake the size of praying hands. You bought dirty yellow coke from a Hells Angel prospect who assaulted girls in tents at festivals. That's how low to the ground you were, kissing broken glass. You sold ket for a white caveman called Super Bitch, and even though this giant maniac kicked someone to death and burgled rich people's homes while they slept, Super Bitch always got away with a suspended sentence. But that's all dead grass now. Since your death, I have adapted the way I eat to work around the rotten wisdom tooth on my left and the shattered bicuspid on my right. The train that cries all night behind the church writes better poems and leaves all the mush and cruelty out. I'm frying eight sausages at one o'clock in the morning, that's how worried I am. Rolling them back and forth across a spitting pan that isn't even mine. Nothing is. Not even my arm. The one with your name on. Twelve years later and this botched ink still itches. Instructions say cook on medium heat for 18-20 minutes. I'm not going anywhere. I'm staying right here with spitting meat. O brother in hell, tell them how the ghosts of your fingers glide through your family's unwashed hair. I press down with the spatula until clear fat squirts up the wall and it's kind of glorious in my fragile state. Eight burning peckers. I'm gonna puke my little guts out. Listen to them sing.

## *Punxsutawney Phil Predicts an Early Spring*
*for Katy*

You're going to think I'm nuts but I swear
I just witnessed a herd of fallow deer
being attacked by *the air*.

Maybe one of them farted.
Mystery over.

God I miss hotels.

          I miss
hugging you in lifts.

When this Groundhog Day is over
I reckon I'm gonna kiss you
like a penny falling into
a very deep well.

## *Power Cut*


They found Micky's decomposing body under a pile of muddy rags in his lonely bedsit, gross on a yellow mattress, wide eyes staring at the wall. My dad regrets kicking the door down to find Micky like that, his oldest friend, rotting in his famous denim jacket. As for me, I was basically suicidal at the time. I didn't think I could help when mom called to say my dad is broken. She was pacing the living room when I got there, yelling, 'Talk to your son!' I shifted closer to him on the sofa. 'All gone now,' he sighed. 'Micky was the last one.' I tried to think of something to say as his bloodshot gaze switched to a different channel. It was The Dead Friends Show and in this special episode there was a power cut on the outskirts of heaven, Micky was prowling the clouds, and the angels were panicking. My mom hovered in the dim yellow light of the hallway as if that's what she was put on this earth to do. Dad clamped his hand on my arm, gently shaking it. He said, 'I'm sick of going to funerals.' I hugged him. He felt so small and empty without his mates. Mom must have boiled the kettle a million times. It was pissing it down outside. I walked home with a tearstained impression of dad's face on my shirt. For some reason I wanted to preserve it. I tried to shield it from the rain. I spent the whole journey pretending to be someone else. Someone with the power to do something to radically affect the lost and barely living. Someone who could talk to the dead. By the time I got home I had almost forgotten the details of my own life, until I noticed the bin was overflowing and I'd left my chores to fester. Then I remembered everything - our shitty doctors and my shoddy brain, how rotten and chicken soupy they can be, and how, when I was growing up, my dad only ever woke me twice in the middle of the night, and that was when his parents died. When his mother slipped away he came into my room, sobbing like a janitor's mop on my new Ghostbusters jumper, 'My mommy, my mommy...' When grandad passed a few years later he wailed, 'My daddy, my daddy...' Just me and him, in the council house dark. That was a bad year, life-changing trauma and such. I had wooden bunk beds at the time, switching from top to bottom whenever I pleased. I swear the beds would shake for no reason sometimes, rattling the ladder like a Disney skeleton's arms. I heard crispy old witches whispering in the walls as our neighbour, the vampire, burned his piano on the lawn. Every now and then, when his girlfriend kicked him out, Micky would crash at our place. He would take the bottom bunk after a massive piss up. It didn't bother me. He was the only family my dad really had. I wish the old man didn't have to find him like that. He talks about those staring eyes and that awful dead brother smell. It's with deep fondness I recall Micky's grizzled snore disturbing my dreams. And since I couldn't get back to sleep, I would lean carefully over the railings and whisper the secret shame of my young life, knowing full well Micky was too fucked up to remember anything I said.

## *Scum of the Earth*

Don't move! I've heard there's a clown
hiding under your bed. Maybe two
clowns, tops. The others are missing.
Please calm down, there's a task force.
Cartoon sirens   *Honker… Honker…*
Do their white gloves squeak
when they rub their hands together?
Look at me, listen… Can they bite
through memory foam? Heaven knows
lonely boys burned so bright and hateful
in my arms, I thought my heart was cooked.
*Oh sweetie, I lost count.* You lost count
of the CLOWNS! Poppy House nods
as Bog Daddy creeps by the window
on   freaking    *killer*     stilts.

## *The State of Sunday*

Mom  I used to know everybody on this estate…

Nan  They're all dead now.

*Grandad puts too much salt on his overcooked beef, reminding me of killing slugs. The salt shaker looks like Donald Duck.*

Grandad  Well, you know I'm an atheist.
I believe in reincarnation.

Me  What if you come back as a Dung Beetle?

Grandad  The human soul wouldn't fit inside
a Dung Beetle.

Me  I thought you said you were an atheist!

Mom  Your dad will be back from the pub soon.

Me  Is he working this week?

Mom  Yeah, just about. He says they're dismantling
the looms.

*Dad was recently made redundant from the carpet factory, along with my uncle, cousin, godfather and most of my dad's friends.*

Grandad　　　　　　　　　　Kidderminster is D E A D

Me　　　　　　　Kitty and I heard weird noises last night.
　　　　　　　　　　　I reckon we've got a poltergeist.

Nan　　I saw lots of ghosts when I worked at the *hospickle*
　　　　　　the really scary ones looked like your grandad!

*Nan is trying to nail an impression of a monster with bits of carrot in her teeth. Grandad is disappointed that I haven't quit smoking. He pulls a face when he notices the picture of a nasty lung on my open pouch. I want to tell mom about the guns and knives I buried behind the shed when I was in high school. I wonder what old weapons look like after all that time in the earth. Do you think the gun still shoots?*

Mom　　　　　It's not the same as it was. They're all gone.

Me　　　　　　Do you remember when you were young?

Nan　　　　　　　　　　　　　　　　Dung Beetles?

# *MEN WITH VEN*

>  'You're not just a man any more, you are a man with a van'
>  — Peep Show

So the new neighbours finally decided
to move in. I watch the removal men
piss about on their drive, punching
leaves on the palm tree, big hands
down their joggers, rummaging
while they wait for the vans to back up.
Then they move, unloading sofas
with their dick fingers and ball stink
over the pillows and mattresses.
I must remember not to mention this
when I meet the new neighbours.
It will be hard, lord knows I'm weird.
I have this built in impulse to shock.
Strange things bother me sideways
and I can't help myself, it's ridiculous.
But if I can keep my mouth shut
this might be our chance to try again.
Just be normal for once. So their house
is tainted with cock - isn't everything?
Don't think about it. Welcome them
with cake and neighbourly behaviour.
No dicks. Say it with me, No. Dicks.
They're going… Going… Gone.

## *Night of the Creeps*

The night my daughter was born I got shit-faced with my dad after nine months of sobriety. He kept saying, 'Aren't you sad it wasn't a boy, son?' Later, as we staggered home, he said this: 'I'm glad I didn't have girls. I'd worry about men trying to fuck them when they're older.' *Sufferin' Succotash!* I tried to write a funny version of this, a poem where no one I love gets hurt. But it's been haunting me lately. His lack and wild misogyny. I will never come out to him. My daughter walks to school on her own now. I dragged my feet as long as I could. It was the only reason I had to leave the house. Holding her cold hand with my warm hand. Pointing at every cat we see and feeling happier for seeing it. We bought a personal alarm on a keyring for her rucksack. Do you know how loud these things are? This one is silver and glittery with a built-in torch that's brighter than it looks. I haven't given it to her yet, though. God damn it I've been meaning to. I guess I just keep forgetting.

# *Catfish Gumbo*
*i.m. Leanne Bridgewater*

Okay, snow is better than me at basketball. It's better at chaos and looking pretty outside. The sweeter the coffee, the sadder the service station. To whoever keeps blow-drying our prizewinning grandmas I'm begging you to stop. I love you like decaying seaside amusements (even the cheating claws). This is the worst picture ever taken of me. I met a horse with a moustache. Sorry for dropping your heart-shaped pie, what a satisfying splat! I'll never get over how pretty. What's the most wtf thing you've seen at the gym? Homemade lemon donuts with white chocolate ganache. Uh, did your cat just shape-shift? To the funny person who painted *Cinderella by day, Sinderella by night* on the side of my caravan THANK YOU!!! Bitch I love it! The earth is currently 100 seconds to midnight on the Doomsday Clock. I noticed the milkman cult are up to their creamy tricks again. I finally found a budgeting technique that works for me: Simulate life, for better or worse. Bounce your dreams off the bad town glitch and watch their makeup shiver.

## *Bottomless Roast*

I'm sorry I can't meet you down the pub today. If I get buzzed I'll smoke weed and have a panic attack. I won't be able to keep my mouth shut about the nonce in the black leather jacket who sits in the middle of the lounge, surrounded by ghoulish old bastards who laugh like Jeff Bezos, and no one does anything about it as I barely contain the urge to glass him. When I get home I will force myself to have a nap even though it's only four o'clock and you know I can't sleep. I just lie there with an unlocked mind opening and closing like a demonstration of a healthy hand: how to punch, how to slap, how to grip the edge. It would be nice to see you; it would be nice to be with that version of you that is possibly the happiest, when you're six pints deep and your sad bloodshot eyes rest upon my face so gently I feel I could hug you but always think better of it. It's too much for me right now. Rotten mental health and this new medication. It's your pub friends telling me how much weight I've gained, patting my belly and saying it's a shame about my ex. It's the cistern surprise in the stinky Gents, lines of mystery powder hidden under the spare bog roll that I will absolutely bang up my nose and spend the next hour chain-smoking roll ups and reminiscing with my old babysitter, Michelle. I actually feel okay today. Not good or great, just kind of peaceful because I'm not thinking about killing myself in a hotel room any more. I just don't want anything to ruin this moment of grace. A calm breeze sweeping through the house seems like God to me, if God is not wanting to harm yourself. If God is planning to cut the grass because cutting the grass will make everything better and my daughter can play outside again. I stare at weeds growing through the holes in the abandoned swing ball rackets left there since the heatwave. The never-used tent, smashing itself against the trees. You know how much your broken ribs hurt right now? Well imagine that's your mind. But I want you to know I almost put on my best Nike trainers and my light blue hat. I held my keys and tried to bend them in the right direction. You should see me with a lawnmower. It wouldn't make you proud or anything but this time last week it was a nightmare. Mom raced over and grabbed me by the arms, wailing: 'Don't you fucking dare!' I'm sorry dad. I don't even know what you expected of a son. There's always next Sunday or the Sunday after that. Did you wear a mask? I can't picture you with a mask on. I was so frightened of your face, you know. It used to be there all the time.

# *The White Flame*

I made peace with my hair falling out I said go for it itchy
scabby skull I've always wondered what you look like
these are supposed to be blackout curtains but daylight
is projecting a tall white flame on the Prussian blue wall
opposite my bed I forgot how clean a sober vision can be
how bitter angels are when I'm bored their silence
the only thing I want because it is brilliant September
so Sertraline does everybody have to drink all the time
can you all stop being drunk for just one minute
I want to tell you something God put the bleeding
glass down look at me I need to talk to you about
cognitive dissonance my daughter growing up and how
unreasonably woebegone that is you can get off your tits
anytime you want sometimes she doesn't talk to me
we sat in the backseat of the taxi of sadness together
I said you're quiet today baby are you okay a dog went by
some flowers a cat on a broken wall the stuff she used to
get excited about I use multi-action eye wash and listen
to classical music my neighbours opening cans of beer
like six gardens away how can I describe the tall white
flame is this a normal level of serotonin kind of a nan vibe
saint of ominous discord teetotal with a benevolent boner
spider season daddy with all the toilet paper in the world
my baseball cap floating in the river the kindness of empty.

# *Revenge is a Dish Best Served Bald*

I spent the best part of a year searching for Cider John. I knew harming him wouldn't change his behaviour. It wouldn't change what he did to Kitty. Nevertheless, I was consumed with disturbing fantasies. Our new cat scratched my hand, and I encouraged her to be more vicious. I ran past his usual haunts every day until I didn't have the energy for revenge. Coming home sweaty and taking it out on my paintings. I was just starting to lose my hair. I even lost some weight. We lived in a gloomy old house by the park. From the dining room window I watched a mad corridor of trees twitch and convulse until our sad nights soaked them. I threw punches at invisible assailants in the smoke-yellowed room where the former tenant died with a skull full of tumours. I tried sobriety for the 100th time but the things it showed us made too much sense and we had to make them stupid again. When I finally confronted Cider John he was walking through town with his asthmatic wife. I followed them past the derelict old courthouse and into the horrible underpass. I booted the discarded takeaways of Saturday morning, scattering greasy bones and stained napkins to get their attention. 'I've been searching for you, John.' I said. They dropped their shopping bags in unison, nasty bottles chiming on the gum-spotted slabs. They didn't seem surprised at all. I realised this was something people said to them all the time. Once I clocked his horrible face, and quickly weighed his desperate nature against my own, I knew I was a coward. I asked if he remembered attacking my partner. John said she must be crazy. 'Yeah,' His wife said. 'She's fucking crazy.' What was I supposed to do? I wanted to frighten him the way he frightened Kitty, and countless other women. But I just walked away. Of course

I did. You have to, don't you? I can still hear my childhood mates calling me a pussy. I suppose they'll always be there, hooting in the haunted woods of twisted masculinity. I've been living in denial of Kitty's prodigious pain for so long. There's nothing I can do. I hold her when she screams. Sometimes I just stare at the floor like one of mother's creepy dolls. Depression was brutal that winter. When I kissed my wrists with the cherry of a spliff the dogs in me stopped barking. At night, I played it over and over again: Cider John in that stinking underpass. His horrified wife and her sad little bags. This useless violence in my hands. All the goddamn Cider Johns of this world. Forgive me, I created a monster in the gloomy garage where poems and paintings lean against the walls like worn-out surgeons. I feed it endless scraps of pure agony until its dark belly is swollen and shiny with hurt. It chuckles and snorts behind the padlocked door while we smoke ourselves senseless. One day it will be strong enough to work for me. Perhaps I'm damned for that. I read somewhere that men get greater satisfaction from witnessing painful retribution whereas women see it as pointless. Do you think that's true? I'm sort of saintly when it comes to waiting. O my bald days, what are they for? Our bloodthirsty cat, sleeping on her wheelchair. The chick with a broken neck on the lawn.

# *A Haunting in Kidderminster*

The bus is on fire again. I watch it burn as I make tea. Why I drink tea at all I don't know. I'm extremely sensitive to caffeine. Decaf tastes like an empty hotel room, a place where people go to stain the sheets. Coming from a family of smokers, I must have reeked of cigarettes as a child. I haven't spoken to my family for months because I realised I'm autistic and they really fucked me over. Jesus, the guilt! The bus makes you think about all sorts of weird things. One day I won't be here to watch it burn. What will happen to the bus then? The bus is always cooking but it's never completely cooked. I wonder if this town is going to wake up and join the dots. What do they think about when they fall asleep? There are fewer people and I've given up on trying to fix them. When I was innocent on the bus before it was burning, everyone thought I was a girl. Look at us now, practically cremated. I guess heaven is a dead bunch of flowers. Sometimes I think I should be less scary. Do people think I'm not scary enough? There's less and less to recognise. If anyone is reading this, I'm not sure what I'll be like when the bus finally burns out. Maybe I won't feel like a monster anymore. I'm not sure if the fire is healing the bus or if the bus is healing the fire. I banged my head against the wall of the mother of visions. I broke the world record for holding your breath. It was awful. It felt like a slow walk home.

## *Honey Monster*

> *Challenge your workmates to the plaster bag strength test. When they lift the bag of dry plaster over their head, cut the underside of the bag, letting the plaster spill out onto them.*
> — Classic Builders Prank

How many people have I killed, almost killed, or harmed without my knowledge? Ugh, who knows. It's all ketchup and milkshake. Black smoke in the break room of my cracked skull factory. I can tell you that some of them went out with a bang, others took their sweet time, like it was our last day on the beach before going home. I could tell you how the dark blood snaked out of their wounds like underwater ink, spreading slowly upward, blocking out the sun. I could tell you that, when I was a kid, death was the only game that truly thrilled me. Killing imaginary people. Picturing them, guts hanging out, screaming for their lives. *Hey mom, I'm an emotional billionaire, stop calling!* Oh well, it doesn't matter if you lose count every now and then. Happens to the best of us. Even survivors forget the odd imaginary slaughter. It comes with the territory. You know that saying, 'Dropping like flies'? Yeah, the world is full of bug spray, and what do we do? We litter window sills with our dried out corpses while they sell us the sticky dreams of blood-drinking suits. Anyway, I looked it up and the origin of this saying is, unfortunately, unknown. I guess it's an allusion to the transitory and fragile nature of an insect's life. I used to believe they were pointless. It's amazing how much a bit of research can do for the planet, and for your soul, which is simply your favourite cartoon before someone thought to draw it. People do fucked up things. Nothing we do is going to change that. Take the worst of them and feed their toxic bodies to the gnarly wood-chipper behind the burned out barn of your imagination. The earliest printed mention of dropping like flies could be this description from The Atlantic Constitution newspaper (May 1902): "I saw men and women rushing back and forth within the flames. They would run along, then came the choking smoke and they would drop like dead flies."

+

Flies make me think about the time I came *this close* to voluntary manslaughter.

Sometime in the early 2000s I started doing odd labouring work for a bad-tempered maniac called Henry. I had no choice. I needed to supplement my sickness benefits. My girlfriend and I often went days without electricity. Henry had his name stencilled on the side of his white Mercedes van, hovering above a grinning cartoon man - one hand stroking your living room wall, the other holding a hawk with a small blob of shit-coloured plaster dripping off the edge. Henry would tell me that he didn't think I had any balls. It was his mantra, 'Bobby no balls... Bobby no balls...'. He said it so often I started believing it. I didn't have balls in a symbolic, spineless way, and the balls I did have were somehow foreign and unnecessary. I could genuinely sense their absence. I still feel completely overwhelmed by their alien attachment to my soft, cowardly body. He knew I was desperate. That's why he worked me so hard and paid such a pathetic wage (off the books, of course). I was a builder's bargain. A shy, malleable addict. Low self-esteem. Pretty, in a certain horrified light, like an abandoned pushchair in the fog. The day I almost took his life, I was sweeping up and trying to look busy, which is difficult when you're stuck in the same gutted room together. Moving through cracked open spaces like traumatised dogs. Gagging on chemicals and farts. Henry was kneeling on a fresh dust sheet with his back to me, screaming till his thick neck turned bright red: 'Hurry up, faggot! Pass me the fucking hammer!'

Kevin got me that job. I practically begged him. He was always there for me, despite the way I treated him. Kevin loved me, he was like a brother and also my best friend. He didn't just survive his own hazing at the hands of cunts like Henry, he ended up tragically controlled by it. Dishing out twisted punishments on his chronically ill step-kids. Bullying the air with his breath. Kevin noticed the way I was holding the hammer. The way I was bouncing it in my hand, weighing it up. He had this curious look on his face. Maybe he wanted it to happen. I wondered how much blood there would be. How many blows it would take. If brains were easy to get at. As I thought about these terrible things, Henry was getting louder, angrier, more abusive: 'If you don't bring me that hammer in five seconds…'

Legend has it the house we were working on used to be owned by a family of witches before the local parish hounded them out of town. They danced around naked in the moonlight and trained their cats to use the toilet. I used to get an aching boner every time I thought about them. It was a sexy house. Bad things happened there. I'm sensitive to light. The house was situated in a quiet neighbourhood behind the high school field. In my teens boys would meet there to fight on a dead patch of land in the middle of the overgrown garden. Max died in the long grass after one tragic punch. Or was it Mark? They all looked the same. Haircuts and muscles. I watched as the colour drained out of them like leftwing leaflets in the rain. This was Henry's biggest job of the year, at least six months' work, minimum. He was in terrible shape. Drinking ten frothy beers in The Peacock every night, chain smoking, living on gross bacon baps from greasy roadside vans. Henry sent me down the cellar for "a long weight". Yeah, I fell for it. What can I say? I was frightened of the man. Would you believe me if I told you he locked me down there, with no light, for hours? Of course you would. Easily top five panic attacks of all time. A familiar voice, slimy in the dark, convincing.

I took a step towards Henry's head. My knuckles blushed around the hammer's rubber handle. I took another step. It's easier than you think, moving towards atrocity. Henry, animal that he was, sensed a shift in the atmosphere. His hands slowly formed a high bridge on the floor, like a sprinter in the starting position. Was he smiling? I looked at Kevin. He was distracted, lost in the shine of his slow drying masterpiece. Staring as if it was suddenly going to form a mouth-shaped gash in the dark plaster and tell him about his real dad and the truth about his negligent family. The joints in Henry's legs going *pop pop pop*.

Henry told me to dig a hole in the garden. That's it. Nothing specific, no preference for depth or duration. Just dig a fucking hole. 'I'm not paying you to daydream!' he said, scratching his sunburned neck. The house was an absolute wreck, but like most things in the sunshine it was also kind of beautiful. When Henry stood over you it was like being in the shadow of a Marlboro Cowboy billboard. He blocked out the sun. He was the sun and my skin was always burning. Henry belched and barked thick specks of froth at me. 'Get digging, boy!' God I hated him. 'Where?' I groaned, carefully treading between the existing holes as if they were open graves. 'Any-fucking-where! I want blisters, worms, earth in your boots!' Was this my initiation? If I could dig a decent hole would that make him happy? Would it mean I had balls? 'And when you're finished with that hole I reckon you're gonna fill the fucker back in…' He flicked his cigarette into the trees. 'You know what? I might ask you to dig it again! What do you think about that, sweetheart? Shit, look at you, bloody gutless. But if you do what I say, and if you're a really *good girl* with that spade, you can scrub the big yellow buckets and bring me clean water in the morning.'

Henry was hired because the original builder conned the owners out of their life savings. Rumour has it he died of a heart attack after a massive crack binge while speeding on a scooter in Thailand. His passenger, a sex worker, survived the crash and arranged a modest funeral. She used the rest of his money to transition, which I really hope is true. One day I heard Henry talking on the phone. His voice sounded kinder than usual. 'Don't worry, sweetheart. Danny got what he deserved. Your house is in good hands now.' It was a beautiful day. The breeze came in through glassless windows, gently pestering the fluffy edges of exposed insulation. The house had a dreamy echo that carried every bump and creak. It smelled like a brand new coffin. But the bumpy ground in the yard was solid. When I slammed the spade into the nasty earth a buried slab announced itself with a sharp jolt through the handle. Henry's face appeared like a rotting joint of ham in the kitchen window. I could see him mouthing those familiar words at me, 'Bobby no balls! You're doing it wrong!' He opened the sliding doors and jabbed a bandaged finger in my direction. 'Fucking DIG!' I looked down on doll heads, roots, bones that somebody loved. Whatever. I was just killing time, waiting for someone to love me the way Henry loved holes.

HAMMER
HAMMER
HAMMER
HAMMER
HAMMER
HAMMER
HAMMER

Can you hear him?

I couldn't see beyond the violent act, but I couldn't work my way around it. My insides were howling. Last night's evil pizza wriggled through my guts like a rat trapped under a blanket. I noticed a new fist-shaped hole in the kitchen wall. Kevin had a short fuse. When his sister was touched in the park, he beat the guy half to death with his skull-shaped motorcycle helmet. Henry taught him everything he knew. Even the patterns of their sunburns were the same. The loving way they hated each other. A shiny pair of tools.

I couldn't see Henry's face, only the back of his angry head. It was like he wasn't a real person to me any more. I get this way when I think about the people who have wronged me. The light goes out of them, leaving baggy costumes full of black wires and burning wind. How many enemies have you slaughtered in your mind, only to bring them back from the dead so you can do it all over again?

Henry was like a biblical figure from a parallel universe where the son of God was a furious ginger plasterer. He had this curious way of holding the ceiling up, using one arm and his square head, shiny tacks tucked between his cracked lips, waiting to be plucked and slugged into the joists using one deft whack of the hammer. He was king of plaster boards and hangover balance. In high school they thought I was a psycho. In a messed up way it made me feel special. Life is a creature feature, after all. I couldn't figure out if I was the monster or the victim.

Kevin saved up for a pair of aluminium plastering stilts. Every morning he would sit on a wooden stool, farting and telling awful jokes, while I strapped the stilts to his chunky legs. 'Nah, that's too tight! Nah, that's loose! Start again, kid.' It was funny at first, watching him learn how to walk - the tick tack noise on the bare floor, and me, awkwardly following, arms outstretched either side of his burly body in case he fell and broke his neck. He looked so cute and pleased with himself, staggering up and down the room that first time. It was like Christmas morning if Christmas morning was someone else's empty house.

*Ten years later.*

*Henry cleaned his one-bedroom flat for the last time.*

*He emptied the bins, ironed his clothes and gathered his life savings, arranging it in neat stacks on the glass coffee table.*

*It didn't amount to much.*

*Then he Googled: How to make a perfect noose.*

*I wonder if he knew his daughter would be the one to find him?*

I had a cramp in my stomach. Henry said the bathroom hadn't been plumbed in yet. He gave me a yellow bucket and pointed to the garage. 'When you're finished,' he grinned. 'Bury it in the garden.' He tossed me a copy of yesterday's paper to wipe with. It was actually a really nice garage. But the fumes from some spilled paint made me feel sick. Henry in bits outside the garage door. Kevin blowing raspberries.

I've never been good at mixing
I couldn't get the ratio right
if the muck was lumpy
Henry would lose his shit
if it was too sloppy
he threw a latter at me
over-mix and the plaster
sets too quick
but the most difficult part
was avoiding

# s  p  l  a  t  t  e  r

Henry's daughter fell in love with a coke dealer. When they were busted, the gang he worked for threatened to set her family's house on fire unless she took the blame. When Henry talked about her it was as if a small tornado of sticks and ashes twirled behind his bloodshot eyes. Perhaps he gave me a hard time because he was trying to help me become more assertive. Sure. I can still picture him sitting in the corner of the rundown social club, running his mouth, laying it on, thick, to my gobsmacked family. 'Your lad's a wimp, you know. He doesn't have any balls. Look at him…'

Tell 'em
        about
   the honey
mummy

he chain-smoked

# SUPER KINGS

Where do you put a beast like Henry? His ghost and the sound of falling tools. I conjure him in the burned out house at the top of the hill with deep yellow buckets, a master's hawk and shrivelled condoms hanging like angels of sadness on the bone-white branches in the yard. His wife, Norma, is there too. She smiles all day long, expertly stripping what's left of the hideous wallpaper. Love songs from the 50s gurgling upstairs from a paint-splattered radio in the cellar. Henry and Norma are going to be there for a long time. Kevin can visit too, if he likes. He can even call them mom and dad. If they're lucky, their daughter might walk by in various stages of her tragic life, dropping shoes, fake roses, dirty pictures. And maybe, just maybe, she will see them every now and then. She will look up and they will be there, flickering in and out of this dimension, waving madly in the window as she giggles in the late autumn fog.

I studied Henry while we ate our lunch: lumpy, scowling, thin lips, ears like Yorkshire puddings. Beer belly, powerful arms, thick fingers with cracks, cuts and calluses. Huge fingernails with blackened blisters and broken skin. We would sit on plastic crates, facing each other. I felt like a man, or what I thought was a man, while eating sandwiches in the rubble of a half-built yard in silence with Henry. Body aching. Buzzing on my brain's finest chemicals, rewarded, drenched in the pride of a day's hard graft. Although, of course, he thought the way I handled my food was too feminine. Henry's bright red hair was like a Pagan ritual headdress or a fistful of matchsticks in a melting Waxwork hand. His pinkish skin, sore from working in the sun, was beet red near the tip of his nose. It was always the same: bacon, egg and sausage sandwiches. Heartburn. Eggy fingers. When he was finished he would ball up the paper bag and the foil and toss them into a nearby bucket. I tried it too, but only the once. He studied me as I scrunched the foil and the greasy paper. I missed the bucket both times. Henry slapped me on the back hard enough to make me cough, then he stood up, belched and called me a faggot. I'm sorry but not one person told me how tough it was going to be. If my family expected me to spend the rest of my life in the company of beasts, the least they could have done is told me about the size of their teeth.

when plaster begins

to darken in colour

its time for the final trowel

nothing is true

when it comes

to relatives

I took another step towards Henry. Sweet Jesus, a hammer never felt so perfect in my hand. I wouldn't blame anyone for thinking I was born with it. Many of us are, we just can't see them until it's too late and someone you thought you hated is seriously hurt, with their shocked blood gushing, spreading across the hardwood floor like a pile of coats. I was the hammer and the hammer was me. I couldn't tell where my flesh ended and the handle began. Perhaps it was a trick of the rubber grip, the texture of it fooling my skin to form a solid connection. Useful and destructive. The flat face that smacks things in and the shiny claw that teases them out. And I was frozen there, in that gutted room, on this violent path, for twenty years.

There's no way I could move on when the anger in my heart still considered itself capable of causing harm to another person when the person in question behaved in a way that made me feel helpless and ashamed. What's that about? At least I got pretty good at digging graves.

Picture a semi-detached, three bedroom house that's been stripped to the bone for refurbishment. The house is situated in a quiet area by the county's oldest church, and even though it's just a stone's throw away from the town's most dangerous council estate, the streets are mostly empty. You'll see that the house is temporarily occupied by a plasterer, his apprentice and an awkward boy with hair like freshly stolen copper. The air is hazy with dust and smoke. It smells like someone died and went to B&Q. Picture crumbling bricks and rough floorboards littered with dollops of dry plaster and flattened cigarette butts, stray tacks and the odd puddle of thick gooey spit (Kevin had a tendency to goz, a nervous habit he picked up as a child). Picture walking through the front door and turning left into the living room. Don't worry, nothing is going to move. I want to show you something. There he is, me, the boy that I was, centre scene, stuck on pause, closing the gap between me and my target, hammer by my side. Henry is motionless too, he looks patient and alert on the wrinkled dust sheet, like he's waiting for the sound of a starting pistol. To your left you'll see Kevin halfway up a stepladder, working on the mantlepiece wall. His shaved head frozen mid-turn, as if he's only just this moment realising his oldest friend is about to snap. Now watch as I turn them into children, into babies, into nothing. Everything must go. There's not even a house. Not even the land on which the house was built.Carbon, oxygen, hydrogen, nitrogen. This whole earthly scene, collapsing through time, back to the glorious source, where Henry can't get you.

I've been carrying these buckets of dirty water for so long, it didn't occur to me that I could just let them go.

I watched the flies crawl over the hammer instead of shaking them off and tossing it into a hole.

I'm tired of digging and I'm sick of Henry's bones in my throat like a handful of pills that won't go down.

What do I want?

I want to be loving awareness.

How much will it cost?

More than the earth.

Am I willing to pay the price?

You bet your sweet ass.

# *Zippo*

I asked the knife to guide me through council estates in the rain. I didn't give a shit about the suffering of animals. I would squint my eyes at teachers and imagine their faces rotting away like B-movie Zombies. I hand-delivered letters to the homes of popular girls who reminded me of the creepy dolls on my mother's bedside table. I faked asthma attacks to get out of sports. The first time I examined my testicles I cried all night, convinced they were full of poisonous, microscopic fish. Doesn't it break your heart when the snow won't stick? Another broken promise. It makes me feel like a witch. When my mom caught me stealing from her purse she dragged me by the hand, screaming, towards the glowing cooker. I walked as slowly as possible up the hill and saw my dad's face in the window like a troubled king, waiting to whip my ass with his leather belt. In all fairness, it didn't hurt a bit; I grinned into the fluffy quilt, thinking about all the other things I could get away with. Once, standing by a river having a piss, enjoying the autumn wind on my skin, a girl appeared carrying a bag filled with muddy high-heeled shoes, which she threw at me. I kept a stash of weapons in my school locker: pellet guns, smoke bombs, knives; I had a reputation for being a little psycho, which was only half true, a phase I hope to purge. The deputy head teacher would make me sit in his office while he ate a whole bunch of large bananas. When a boy called Ryan spat in my face, I followed him to the park where he sat on the grass with his back to me. I took a long run up and kicked his head like a football, knocking him unconscious, then I ran home and hid in my wardrobe, waiting for the police to come and arrest me for murder. Mom told me that boys have a tail and girls have a hole. Nothing about pleasure, connection, intimacy. Just tails and holes. That's it. After my nan died, I watched my grandad slowly lose his mind with grief and whisky. He would scream at the living room wall for days while Pavarotti boomed from the speakers of his dusty radio, drowning out the awful tinnitus he developed during the war. My best friend helped me dig under my grandad's shed searching for dinosaur bones. We found two small skulls, which I cleaned and brought into science class, only to be told they were the remains of cats, hence my short-lived reputation as a cat killer. Thankfully, I discovered poetry, it was my secret; it excited me. I was sent to the warehouse above Marks & Spencer for work experience, where I touched the cold, white breasts of headless mannequins and all I could think about was stealing women's stockings, black, shiny, secretly wearing them as I jerked off in the toilets. But I could never go through with it. I was convinced that every person to ever die and go to heaven was watching me, appalled. Since my dad is a Glazier there were always odd bits of glass laying around the house. His thumbs loosely wrapped with oozing bandages. I enjoyed squishing slugs and snails between two small pieces of broken glass, so that I could see the colours of their insides. Whenever dad left the room I would use his brass Zippo lighter to burn the faces off my favourite action figures. There was a very odd woman who lived down the street, her name was Mandy, she had intense silver eyes and wore pink fluffy jumpers that were way too big for her but made her seem closer to my age at the time. Mandy invited me into her house. The way she growled and licked her lips disturbed me. I took the Dictaphone I got for my twelfth birthday to the local haunted house and propped it up in the fire-damaged kitchen, hoping to catch something supernatural. When I retrieved it the next day the Dictaphone had recorded the voice of a boy begging a girl to suck his dick, the sound of a scuffle, gagging, sobbing. I believed the Devil was playing tricks on me. If I could choose between complete sobriety or self-discipline I would choose the willpower to enjoy drugs occasionally without my life falling apart and disappointing my family. This is subject to change. Do you have to write about yourself to make sense of yourself? I don't know anything about you. Tell me. I'm becoming a real creature of the moment. Have you considered writing a diary from the perspective of your penis? My earliest memory of being truly aware of it, I was sitting on a bed behind the curtains with our family doctor, he was rolling my foreskin up and down for a long time. Right now, it feels creepy-crawly (which always happens when it knows it's being talked about). Hidden in my dad's bedside drawer was a poem he wrote for my mom when she was pregnant with me, in hospital, awaiting chemotherapy for the cancer that appeared in her neck like a hundred baked beans under the skin. He wrote about how he couldn't wait to meet their baby daughter. Perhaps this was the first seed. I had already been through stages when I believed I was an alien, sent to cause chaos. If this is the wrong body, I thought, I'll fucking ruin it. A posh boy who lived in the big house on the hill asked me to use his camcorder to record a video of him masturbating. When I refused, he threw biscuits at the Au Pair until she took off crying down the road and got hit by a bus. I think about her whenever I eat Vegan breakfasts. Early memories, for me, can often be summed up with one chilling sentence. If you had to describe your childhood in terms of food, what lunch would you be? I was a cold Happy Meal. The only time I think about my doomed wedding day, I see my ex-wife and I, posing for pictures in front of St Mary's, the greenish stone archway covered with hundreds of Ladybirds, dropping into her veil and crawling all over her white dress. I guess it was kind of magical. According to legend, in France, if a Ladybird lands on you, whatever ailment you have will fly away with the Ladybird. In some Asian cultures it is believed that Ladybirds understand human language and have been blessed by God. I couldn't consummate the marriage because I was too high on strong biker speed. We watched cartoons until we fell asleep. Do you ever put your thumb in your mouth and run the tip of your tongue across your thumbnail to appreciate how smooth and glassy it is? In some areas, this is a signal to a dark, twisted figure in a second-floor hotel window. Do we really die? I do not recommend loneliness, though I know that many people can enjoy their own company without going slightly insane. I am not one of these people. I slap my own face so hard my teeth rattle. I do this because I feel lost in all the noise of apparent normalcy. The day you were born is essentially the most important thing to happen ever. Remember this when someone tries to convince you to do something disgusting. Remember this when governments fall and wolves are reintroduced to the English countryside. Remember this: your physical presence can be reduced to a drop of digital blood falling through eternal screens. In this I have achieved a small release. I live easier for a while. Maybe I am to blame for the way her life turned out. My passion for drugs was predestined, handed down like a broken watch, inevitable as flies. My heart was like the Bermuda Triangle: birds fell out of the sky and loved ones vanished in the dead of night. When the guilt is really bad it's like my skull picks up all these wild vibrations, echoes, songs, stories, voices, instruments, animal noises, soundtracks to German cinema. In the absence of faith or spirituality (which I once had in abundance) I struggle to see beyond the poorly packaged bacon of existence. My partner tells me science is beautiful and pure. Sometimes I believe her. Now we're past the church. I can't hear anything but rain. I'm jeepers creepers in love again. Is it true you can enter other people's dreams and cast a sickness upon them? I heard people who die angry can become powerful ghosts. I memorised the names of antidepressants as if they were angels. I threw my illness off the ugliest bridge in the world and ran as fast as I could.

# *Acknowledgements*

I would like to thank the following magazines, where earlier versions of the following poems first appeared:

'Floating in the Harbour' — G.O.B. Magazine

'Spooky Jeans' — Bath Magg

'Come Down (Three Bad Dreams)' — Anthropocene

'Zippo' — *The Dizziness of Freedom anthology*, Bad Betty Press

I didn't submit the rest of the pieces in this book because I impulsively posted them on social media as soon as I finished writing them.

Huge thanks to Aaron Kent for publishing *Resurrection Mary* (Secret Sleep Books) as a limited edition pamphlet to raise money for AGE UK, and for being so kind and supportive of my work.

I'm deeply indebted to my partner, Katy Venables, who went through many versions of the manuscript with an expert editorial eye, and helped me bring *Honey Monster* to completion. Without her, everything would be lost.

# LAY OUT YOUR UNREST

Lightning Source UK Ltd.
Milton Keynes UK
UKHW020626080222
398338UK00006B/67